Wrestling fans, this is it! A challenge you can't refuse—The Professional Wrestling Trivia Book. Sharpen your grappling skills in this no-holds-barred workout and contend for the Heavyweight Wrestling Trivia Crown!

Here's the first fall—no time limit:

What character did Hulk Hogan portray in Rocky III?

Is Ric Flair really Jewish?

What do Lex Lugar, Tully Blanchard, and Arn Anderson have in common?

Who heads Titan Sports?

How does Dusty Rhodes sign his name?

Who broke Hillbilly Jim's leg?

What is a "bozark"?

Who was known as Moose Myers?

What is Andre the Giant's shoe size?

The Professional Wrestling Trivia Book

By Robert Myers

Popular Technology
A Division of Branden Publishing Company

Library of Congress Cataloging-in-Publication Data

Myers, Robert, 1947–
   The professional wrestling trivia book / by Robert Myers.
     p. cm. — (Pro wrestling trivia book; 5)
   ISBN 0-8283-1920-0 (pbk.): $7.95
   1. Wrestling—Miscellanea. I. Title. II. Series.
GV1195.M94 1988
796.8'12—dc19   88-22378
                                CIP

Popular Technology
17 Station Street
Box 843 Brookline Village
Boston, MA 02147

TO SKULL MURPHY

wherever you are

Acknowledgments

A book such as this would not be complete without a list of acknowledgments.

In the course of preparing this manuscript numerous references and organizations were consulted. Among them: The Associated Press, *The Guinness Book of World Records*, *Inside Wrestling*, *The National Enquirer*, *Newsweek*, The New York Public Library, *The People's Almanac #1*, *People Magazine*, *Pro Wrestling Illustrated*, *Sports Review Wrestling*, "Sports World" (NBC-TV), *Time Magazine*, "20/20" (ABC-TV), *The Village Voice*, *The World Scope Encyclopedia Yearbook*, *The Wrestler*, *Wrestling*, *Wrestling All Stars*, *Wrestling Eye*, and *Wrestling News*.

I would especially like to thank Adolpho Caso, President of Popular Technology, who guided every phase of this book's development.

Theo Ehret and the late Gene Gordon must be cited for their fine photographic work.

A deep appreciation to my children, Kevin and Lisa, for staying out of the way. And to my wife, Ellen, who understood my need to create. Thanks to their unselfishness, I was able to spend many evenings and weekends on the book—valuable time that rightfully belonged to them.

And lastly, a special word of praise for my parents, Hilda and Joseph W. Myers, whose love and devotion I now fully appreciate.

Contents

Illustrations

Introduction

My addiction to professional wrestling began in the fifties. I guess you can say television made me do it. The program was called "Championship Wrestling" and originated from the old Capitol Arena in Washington, D.C. Sitting comfortably in front of my black and white Philco, I watched the likes of Killer Kowalski, Buddy Rogers, Yukon Eric, and Antonino Rocca do their thing. It was pure magic. I loved it! Wrestling became an obsession. I joined several fan clubs, even had rasslin' pen pals. Words like "body-slam," "footstomp," and "half nelson" crept into my vocabulary. I had indeed transformed myself into a professional wrestling junkie. And now after some three decades and literally thousands of matches, it remains for me as exciting, refreshing, and entertaining as ever.

Most of us are by now familiar with the pro wrestling phenomenon sweeping the country. Thanks to renowned promoter Vince McMahon, Jr., and his World Wrestling Federation, professional wrestling has become respectable. It is big business. There are wrestling dolls, cartoon shows, posters, and merchandise. This year alone over 20 million people will attend matches. Wrestling events are among the highest rated cable/pay TV programs on the air. Nationally, the sport will generate sales in excess of half a billion dollars. For now at least, it looks as if grappling has hit pay dirt.

Fortunately for us, little else has changed within pro grappling. The current "cast of characters" is just as talented, just as mean, just as outrageous as their legendary counterparts. And I've tried to touch on them all, from Gorgeous George to Hulk Hogan, from Bruno Sammartino to Junkyard Dog, and from The Fabulous Moolah to Wendi Richter. They are all here—the good, the bad, and the ugly.

To provide some semblance of order, I have divided this book into parts, i.e., tag teams, legends, women, and so on. The entries appearing in each part are not in any particular order or sequence, but are randomly presented. They span some six decades of ring history and a countless number of wrestlers. In all honesty, I would be very much surprised to discover someone had correctly answered *all* the questions. Should you perform this miraculous feat, let me know. I'll gladly submit your name for candidacy to the Trivia Hall of Fame.

Good luck!

PART I
Heroes
and
Villains

Heroes and Villains

1. What character did Hulk Hogan portray in *Rocky III*?

   a) Man Mountain Dean
   b) Clubber Lang
   c) Hacksaw Wilson
   d) Thunderlips

2. How does Dusty Rhodes sign his name?

   a) Sylvester Ritter
   b) Ed Wiskoski
   c) Virgil Runnels
   d) Dan Frazier

3. AIDS testing is now mandatory in professional wrestling.

   True or False?

4. ..... does the commentary on the WWF's Spanish-language telecasts.

   a) Gene Okerlund
   b) Pedro Alonzo
   c) Miguel Perez
   d) Miguel Alonzo

5. The "Monster Factory" is run by

   a) Killer Kowalski
   b) David Shultz
   c) Johnny Hunter
   d) Larry Sharpe

6. "It will bring out the genius in you" is whose line?

   a) Bam Bam Bigelow
   b) David Shultz
   c) King Kong Bundy
   d) Slick

7. What is a "bozark"?

   a) A midget wrestler
   b) A woman wrestler
   c) A woman midget wrestler
   d) An overweight wrestler

8. Identify the bizarre grappling gladiator from England.

   a) Adrian Street
   b) Mister Blackwell
   c) Johnny Pravos
   d) Barry Starr

9. What popular mat star was offered a Washington Redskin football contract by George Allen?

   a) Hulk Hogan
   b) John Studd
   c) Andre the Giant
   d) Bruno Sammartino

10. Ed Leslie struts his stuff as

   a) The Honky Tonk Man
   b) Brutus Beefcake
   c) Adrian Street
   d) Adrian Adonis

11. A hairy King Kong Bundy went by the moniker

    a) Randy Bundy
    b) Killer Bundy
    c) Chris Canyon
    d) Chic Canyon

12. Who wrote *Pro-Wrestling Finishing Holds?*

    a) Lou Thesz
    b) Buddy Rogers
    c) Gene LeBell
    d) Bob Backlund

13. Ric Flair has recently converted to Judaism.

    True of False?

14. Which of the following is not a professional wrestling organization?

    a) NWA
    b) WWF
    c) WBA
    d) AWA

15. Crusher Yurkov is now

    a) The Honky Tonk Man
    b) Rick Rude
    c) Bam Bam Bigelow
    d) Randy Savage

16. Who succeeded Stan Stasiak as WWF heavyweight champ?

    a) Bruno Sammartino
    b) Billy Graham
    c) Bob Backlund
    d) Ivan Koloff

17. Ruddy Reyna, Rizado Ruiz, and Brazo De Oro are all wrestlers on the Mexican circuit.

    True or False?

18. ..... served as guest timekeeper for Wrestlemania I.

    a) Billy Martin
    b) Joe Frazier
    c) Liberace
    d) Willie Mays

19. This guy's a real ace.

    a) Tommy Rich
    b) Chris Adams
    c) Bob Orton
    d) Terry Gordy

20. Second-generation grapplers include all of the following except

    a) Curt Hennig (Tommy Hennig)
    b) Jake Roberts (Grizzly Smith)
    c) Greg Gagne (Verne Gagne)
    d) Barry Windham (Blackjack Mulligan)

#25: Who was the first man permitted by the New York State Athletic Commission to wear a mask in the ring? (Photo by Theo Ehret)

21. This Blonde Bomber loves rock 'n' roll.

    a) Wayne Ferris
    b) Barry Windham
    c) Ric Flair
    d) Dusty Rhodes

22. "Doctor Death" ..... does not make house calls.

    a) Billy Gilbert
    b) Jim Neidhart
    c) Steve Williams
    d) Les Thornton

23. Tiger Chung Lee a.k.a.

    a) Tiger Skna & Kim Luck
    b) Ruddy Reyna & Kim Duk
    c) Tiger Taguchi & Kim Duk
    d) Tiger Taguchi & Kim Luck

24. Jimmy Hart was an NWA sanctioned referee.

    True or False?

25. Who was the first man permitted by the New York State Athletic Commission to wear a mask in the ring?

    a) Mil Mascaras
    b) The Spoiler
    c) The Masked Marvel
    d) Mr. Wrestling I

26. When was this decision handed down?

    a) 1969
    b) 1979
    c) 1964
    d) 1972

27. Who refereed the title match between Dusty Rhodes and Ric Flair in November 1984?

    a) Joe Frazier
    b) Larry Holmes
    c) Terry Funk
    d) Bruno Sammartino

28. This Minneapolis native began his career in the AWA.

    a) Ric Flair
    b) Kevin Kelly
    c) Barry Windham
    d) Randy Savage

29. What promoter was responsible for Hulk Hogan's early success?

    a) Greg Gagne
    b) Vince McMahon
    c) Freddie Blassie
    d) Verne Gagne

30. *Body Slam* did not showcase

    a) Randy Savage
    b) The Tonga Kid
    c) Konga the Barbarian
    d) Teijho Khan

31. Select the cowboys.

    a) Bob and Scott
    b) Bob and Billy
    c) Billy and Jack
    d) Rick and Jim

32. The life expectancy of a wrestler is greater than that of other athletes.

    True or False?

33. The Iceman Cometh. Who cometh?

    a) King Kong Bundy
    b) King Kong Brody
    c) King Parsons
    d) King Konga

34. ..... executes the camel clutch.

    a) The Iron Sheik
    b) Rick Rude
    c) George Steele
    d) Hulk Hogan

35. How long did Ivan Koloff hold the WWF heavyweight title?

    a) 3 years
    b) 3 months
    c) 3 weeks
    d) 6 months

36. What is Ivan's relationship to Nikita Koloff?

    a) His uncle
    b) His brother
    c) His nephew
    d) His father

37. Who is KKK?

    a) Killer Kevin Krupp
    b) Killer Kerry Kamp
    c) Killer Karl Krupp
    d) Killer Kerry Krupp

38. "The King" sent funnyman ..... to the hospital.

    a) Richard Belzer
    b) David Letterman
    c) Andy Kaufman
    d) Johnny Carson

39. ..... is not family.

    a) Barry
    b) Blackjack
    c) Mike
    d) Kendall

40. David was the eldest son of the legendary great Fritz Von Erich.

    True or False?

41. Ravishing Rick Rude and ..... combined their mat skills to capture the mid-Southern tag team crown.

    a) King Kong Bundy
    b) Bam Bam Bigelow
    c) Steve Williams
    d) Curt Hennig

42. A Slammy Award was given to ..... as Best Body of 1987.

    a) Tony Atlas
    b) Rick Rude
    c) Hercules Hernandez
    d) Lex Lugar

43. A ..... is a masked wrestler.

    a) Stocking
    b) Mark
    c) Plant
    d) Bozark

44. "Saturday Night's Main Event" is basically a showcase for ..... talents.

    a) AWA
    b) WWF
    c) UWF
    d) NWA

45. ..... is Mil Mascaras' brother.

    a) Mike Mascaras
    b) Jerry Martin
    c) Dos Caras
    d) Mil Caras

46. ..... runs a correspondence school of wrestling.

   a) Killer Kowalski
   b) Johnny Valentine
   c) Arnold Skaaland
   d) Bob Backlund

47. ..... is called "The Brandon Bull" after his home town in Florida.

   a) Eddie Gilbert
   b) Paul Orndorff
   c) Randy Savage
   d) Tommy Rich

48. ..... has guided both The One Man Gang and Billy Graham.

   a) Sir Oliver Pumperdinkel
   b) Sir Laurence Oliver
   c) Sir Oliver Humperdink
   d) Sir Oscar Radcliff

49. Buddy Rose and Sergeant Slaughter were both managed by The Grand Wizard.

   True or False?

50. ..... won a 20-man battle royal at Wrestlemania II.

   a) Hulk Hogan
   b) Andre the Giant
   c) Randy Savage
   d) John Studd

51. ..... refused to wrestle Jimmy Snuka "because he's black."

    a) Dusty Rhodes
    b) Jake Roberts
    c) Colonel DeBeers
    d) Tully Blanchard

52. ..... surfaced as The Giant Machine.

    a) King Kong Bundy
    b) Andre the Giant
    c) John Studd
    d) Blackjack Mulligan

53. What pro grappling organization has created Superstars of Wrestling Bars?

    a) NWA
    b) WWF
    c) AWA
    d) UWF

54. ..... became the UWF's initial heavyweight champion.

    a) Terry Taylor
    b) Ted DiBiase
    c) Terry Gordy
    d) Steve Williams

55. Bam Bam Bigelow's mentor was

    a) Larry Sharpe
    b) Killer Kowalski
    c) Bobby Heenan
    d) Vince McMahon

#60: ..... is the native land of Abdullah the Butcher. (Photo by Theo Ehret)

56. The Fabulous Moolah a.k.a.

    a) Lillian Ellison
    b) Lillian Erickson
    c) Helen Morgan
    d) Hilda Erickson

57. Which of the following is not a wrestling hold?

    a) Pile-driver
    b) Half nelson
    c) Window wrap
    d) Clothes-line

58. ..... ("the city that never sleeps") is fast becoming a wrestling mecca.

    a) Atlantic City
    b) Las Vegas
    c) Los Angeles
    d) Toronto

59. ..... appears in a Joe Piscopo film.

    a) Hulk Hogan
    b) Lou Albano
    c) Bruno Sammartino
    d) Bobby Heenan

60. ..... is the native land of Abdullah the Butcher.

    a) Israel
    b) Japan
    c) Brooklyn
    d) The Sudan

61. Who is Betsy?

    a) Ronnie Garvin's valet
    b) Ron Bass' whip
    c) Koko B. Ware's bird
    d) Slick's stick

62. The Spoiler and El Halcon are masked grapplers.

    True or False?

63. The NWA is basically a touring exhibition controlled by

    a) Titan Sports
    b) Jim Crockett Promotions
    c) Jim Cornette Promotions
    d) World Wide Sports

64. What does T.A. stand for in Magnum T.A.?

    a) Tough Ass
    b) Tom Allen
    c) Terry Allen
    d) Taylor Adams

65. Top star attractions of England and Austria are

    a) Wayne Bridges & Otto Wanz
    b) Jan Wilkens & Steve Williams
    c) Micky Duff & Bryan Wilheim
    d) Micky Duff & Wayne Bridges

66. Scott Armstrong is Brad's older brother.

    True or False?

67. ..... fought Muhammad Ali to a draw in a boxing-wrestling exhibition.

    a) Antonio Inoki
    b) Toshiaki Kawada
    c) Masanobu Fuchi
    d) Takachi Ishikawa

68. Randy Savage once met Lanny Poffo in a championship title match.

    True or False?

69. Ex-boxer and now wrestling referee ..... challenged Larry Holmes for the world's heavyweight boxing crown.

    a) Danny Davis
    b) Jim Horner
    c) Tony Galento
    d) Scott LeDoux

70. The running body-slam as practiced by King Kong Bundy is called

    a) The Bundy Bomb
    b) The Los Angeles Quake
    c) The Atlantic City Avalanche
    d) The TNT Blast

71. Bundy's move is reminiscent of

    a) The Rocca Rock
    b) The Texas Tornado
    c) The Oklahoma Stampede
    d) The Sammartino Squat

72. Who did The Iron Sheik defeat to gain the WWF title?

    a) Bruno Sammartino
    b) Andre the Giant
    c) Bob Backlund
    d) Billy Graham

73. Wrestling executive Bob Geigel is associated with what organization?

    a) WWF
    b) NWA
    c) AWA
    d) NCAA

74. What is Shohei Baba's middle name?

    a) Baby
    b) King
    c) King Kong
    d) Giant

75. This entry is incorrect.

    a) Wahoo McDaniel—Midland, TX
    b) Rick Rude—Robbinsdale, MN
    c) Rick Steiner—Vero Beach, FL
    d) One Man Gang—Chicago, IL

76. The Batten Twins are identical.

    True or False?

77. ..... can not be purchased at your newsstand.

    a) *Pro Wrestling Illustrated*
    b) *Grappling News*
    c) *Wrestling Scene*
    d) *Wrestling Eye*

78. Which of the following gentlemen does not have a weight problem?

    a) The Barbarian
    b) Chris Adams
    c) Dusty Rhodes
    d) Kamala

79. Lex Lugar tips the scales at

    a) 268 pounds
    b) 290 pounds
    c) 229 pounds
    d) 249 pounds

80. The WWF has been in existence longer than both the NWA and the AWA.

    True or False?

#87: The motion picture ..... introduced Roddy Piper to Hollywood.
(Photo by Theo Ehret)

81. Former WWF titleholder ..... was also an N.C.A.A. champ.

    a) Bruno Sammartino
    b) Billy Graham
    c) Bob Backlund
    d) Buddy Rogers

82. Sergeant Slaughter's given name is

    a) Gene
    b) Bob
    c) Dave
    d) George

83. "Juice" and ..... are synonymous.

    a) Speed
    b) Sweat
    c) Blood
    d) Heat

84. The video *Time After Time* featured

    a) Hulk Hogan
    b) Michael Hayes
    c) Lou Albano
    d) Roddy Piper

85. Capital Wrestling Corporation was headed by whom?

    a) Vince McMahon, Jr.
    b) Lou Thesz
    c) Don King
    d) Vince McMahon, Sr.

86. Bret Hart is the son of ex-wrestler and Calgary promoter

    a) Blackjack Mulligan
    b) Larry Hart
    c) Stu Hart
    d) Bob Orton, Sr.

87. The motion picture ..... introduced Roddy Piper to Hollywood.

    a) *The Predator*
    b) *The Harder They Fall*
    c) *Body Slam*
    d) *The Last Match*

88. Hulk Hogan claims to have ..... inch pythons.

    a) 18
    b) 24
    c) 28
    d) 30

89. A grappler's ..... is his routine.

    a) Mouthpiece
    b) Stocking
    c) Shtick
    d) Marshmallow

90. Where was Andre the Giant born?

    a) Paris
    b) Grenoble
    c) London
    d) Iceland

91. WWF President ..... revoked Danny Davis' official's license for life.

    a) Verne Gagne
    b) Jack Tunney
    c) Gene Tunney
    d) Vince McMahon

92. What do Bam Bam Bigelow and King Kong Bundy have in common?

    a) Birthdays
    b) Parents
    c) Alma maters
    d) Residences

93. Which of the following is incorrect?

    a) Bubba Rogers: 348 pounds, Hendersonville, TN
    b) Kevin Kelly: 271 pounds, Oakland, CA
    c) Black Bart: 261 pounds, Pampa, TX
    d) Steve Williams: 265 pounds, Norman, OK

94. Gorgeous Keith Franks is currently grappling under the moniker

    a) Buddy Roberts
    b) Ted DiBiase
    c) Adrian Adonis
    d) Chris Adams

95. Mr. Wonderful has recently teamed up with his dad, Troy Orndorff.

    True or False?

96. Who was described as "the ultimate mountain of desire"?

   a) Hulk Hogan
   b) Terry Funk
   c) John Studd
   d) Man Mountain Dean

97. What cities hosted Wrestlemania II?

   a) San Francisco, Chicago, New York
   b) Detroit, Chicago, Los Angeles
   c) New York, Chicago, Los Angeles
   d) New York, Chicago, Miami

98. "The New Bruce Lee" matches up with

   a) The Cheetah Kid
   b) Tonga Kid II
   c) Ricky Steamboat
   d) Vince Apollo

99. Vince McMahon, Jr. heads up the organization known as

   a) ESPN
   b) Titan Sports
   c) MSG
   d) Top Rank

100. The word "broadway" refers to a grappling

   a) Count out
   b) Bout
   c) Disqualification
   d) Draw

#107: Rocky Johnson is taller than Mr. T. True or False? (Photo by Theo Ehret)

101. While taping a segment for ABC-TV's "20/20," an investigative reporter was slugged by

    a) Hulk Hogan
    b) Jerry Lawler
    c) David Shultz
    d) Mr. T.

102. ..... was the unfortunate newsman.

    a) Jim Jensen
    b) John Stossel
    c) Richard Belzer
    d) Jack Reynolds

103. What question infuriated the grappler?

    a) Are you gay?
    b) Is wrestling fake?
    c) Is your marriage breaking up?
    d) How much money do you make?

104. Vince McMahon's wrestling organization was previously known as

    a) WWWF
    b) WIF
    c) WWA
    d) UWF

105. V.V. is a Brooklyn boy.

    a) Victor Valentino
    b) Vinnie Valentino
    c) Vinnie Victor
    d) Victor Vachon

106. "Polish Power" is music to the ears of

 a) Ivan Pitkofsky
 b) Warner Polanski
 c) Ivan Putski
 d) Igor Polanski

107. Rocky Johnson is taller than Mr. T.

 True or False?

108. ..... were a celebrated father-son combo.

 a) The Funks
 b) The Hogans
 c) The Rhodes'
 d) The Lawlers

109. "Grab Them Cakes" has been most closely identified with

 a) Butch Reed
 b) Slick
 c) Junkyard Dog
 d) Tony Atlas

110. Heredity is the key to this grappler's success.

 a) George Steele
 b) Ted DiBiase
 c) Dusty Rhodes
 d) Ric Flair

111. ..... is a bit out of place here.

   a) Paul Orndorff
   b) Lex Lugar
   c) Dusty Rhodes
   d) Kevin Von Erich

112. ..... is the senior editor of *Pro Wrestling Illustrated*.

   a) Ken Morgan
   b) Vince McMahon
   c) Bill Apter
   d) Stanley Harris

113. "Pomp and Circumstance" greets the arrival of

   a) Harley Race
   b) Jerry Lawler
   c) Randy Savage
   d) Roddy Piper

114. ..... is the self-proclaimed "Universal Heartthrob."

   a) Adrian Street
   b) Austin Idol
   c) Buddy Rose
   d) Dusty Rhodes

115. What musical instrument does Hulk Hogan play?

   a) Guitar
   b) Piano
   c) Clarinet
   d) Trumpet

116. ..... died from a heart attack while engaged in a match.

   a) David Von Erich
   b) King Cobra
   c) Iron Mike DiBiase
   d) Antonino Rocca

117. "The Wrestler Who Made Milwaukee Famous"

   a) Jerry Lawler
   b) Ric Flair
   c) Greg Valentine
   d) The Crusher

118. The LWA translates into

   a) The Ladies Wrestling Association
   b) The Ladies Wrestling Alliance
   c) The Liberty Wrestling Alliance
   d) The Lambda Wrestling Alliance

119. What is the tie that binds Gene Louis, Lanny Keenan, and Dan Frazier?

   a) They are hillbillies
   b) They are midgets
   c) They wear masks
   d) They are referees

120. When did Bob Backlund commence his great pro wrestling career?

   a) 1960
   b) 1964
   c) 1974
   d) 1970

121. Select the mismatch.

    a) Ivan & Scott Putski
    b) Paul & Troy Orndorff
    c) Jerry & Terry Lawler
    d) Barry & Kendall Windham

122. Super Destroyer ..... put on a mask as Super Machine.

    a) Adrian Street
    b) Rip Rogers
    c) Robert Gibson
    d) Bill Eadie

123. The promotion which saw Mr. T. come to the aid of Cyndi Lauper and Hulk Hogan was called

    a) The Brawl To End It All
    b) Super Sunday
    c) Wrestlemania I
    d) The War To Settle The Score

124. What is Hugo Savinovich's connection with women's wrestling?

    a) He discovered Wendi Richter
    b) He married Wendi Richter
    c) His sister is The Fabulous Moolah
    d) He founded the IWWA

125. Ronnie and Jimmy Garvin are in no way related.
    True or False?

126. In Wrestlemania I, ... pinned ..... in a record-breaking 13 seconds.

    a) Bam Bam Bigelow, Bruno Sammartino, Jr.
    b) Bam Bam Bigelow, Koko B. Ware
    c) King Kong Bundy, S.D. Jones
    d) King Kong Bundy, Bruno Sammartino, Jr.

127. He is America's hero.

    a) Hulk Hogan
    b) Sergeant Slaughter
    c) Ric Flair
    d) Dusty Rhodes

128. She kissed Ted DiBiase good night.

    a) Helen Hild
    b) Alice DiBiase
    c) Helen Moore
    d) Judy Martin

129. ..... and Crocodile Dundee have much in common.

    a) Jake Roberts
    b) Andre the Giant
    c) Outback Jack
    d) Adrian Street

130. Todd Okerlund, the son of veteran wrestling announcer Mean Gene Okerlund, is a member of the U.S. Olympic ..... team.

    a) Basketball
    b) Hockey
    c) Wrestling
    d) Swimming

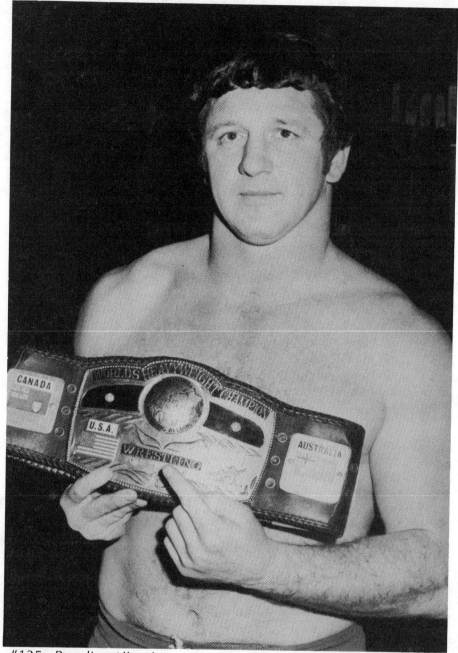

#135: *Paradise Alley* featured what pro grappler? (photo by Gene Gordon)

131. ..... was the idol of ..... .

    a) Bruno Sammartino, Roddy Piper
    b) Verne Gagne, Ric Flair
    c) Buddy Rogers, Ric Flair
    d) Johnny Valentine, Jake Roberts

132. What event did not take place during Wrestlemania II?

    a) Hogan vs Bundy in steel cage
    b) Studd wins 20-man battle royal
    c) Savage defeats Steele
    d) Mr. T over Piper by disqualification

133. Moose Myers has transformed himself into

    a) George Steele
    b) Adrian Adonis
    c) Randy Savage
    d) Bubba Rogers

134. A ..... is a wrestler disguised as a "mark" and planted in the audience.

    a) Jobber
    b) Plant
    c) Bozark
    d) Stocking

135. *Paradise Alley* featured what pro grappler?

    a) Hulk Hogan
    b) Roddy Piper
    c) Terry Funk
    d) Greg Valentine

136. ..... is a bowwow.

    a) Ed Leslie
    b) Terry Allen
    c) LeRoy Wilson
    d) Sylvester Ritter

137. Which of the following individuals has not written a book on professional wrestling?

    a) Robert Myers
    b) Gene LeBell
    c) Burt Sugar
    d) John Boyer

138. Who is the heaviest?

    a) Hulk Hogan
    b) Bruiser Brody
    c) Dusty Rhodes
    d) Crusher Blackwell

139. Prior to his emergence as a WWF mat star, Hillbilly Jim had no professional wrestling experience.

    True or False?

140. The Honky Tonk Man and ..... are cousins.

    a) Jerry Lawler
    b) Tommy Rich
    c) Ron Bass
    d) Eddie Gilbert

141. ..... does not belong.

   a) Krusher Khrushev
   b) Smash
   c) Barry Darsow
   d) Vladimir Pietrov

142. Superstar and Superbrat are really

   a) John Studd & Greg Valentine
   b) Billy Graham & Dusty Rhodes
   c) Jerry Graham & Dusty Rhodes
   d) Billy Graham & Tully Blanchard

143. How many fans turned out to see Wrestlemania III?

   a) 57,000
   b) 157,000
   c) 93,000
   d) 73,000

144. Where was this historic exhibition staged?

   a) Madison Square Garden
   b) Yankee Stadium
   c) Pontiac Silverdome
   d) Texas Stadium

145. ..... was the first (and only) Hispanic to hold the WWF heavyweight crown.

   a) Pedro Morales
   b) Carlos Colon
   c) Pedro Martinez
   d) Hercules Hernandez

146. ..... and free-style wrestling are equivalent.

    a) Sumo wrestling
    b) Greco-Roman wrestling
    c) Judo-grappling
    d) Catch-as-catch-can

147. There is only one ..... , the Black Ninja.

    a) Kendo Morti
    b) Miki Moto
    c) Kendo Moto
    d) Kendo Nagazaki

148. This gentleman is an outlaw.

    a) Jim Duggan
    b) Jimmy Garvin
    c) Ron Bass
    d) Shane Douglas

149. Who serves as publisher for the WWF's official publication?

    a) Linda Kelly
    b) Nina McMahon
    c) Linda Moore
    d) Jack Kelly

150. A ..... is a TV bum or preliminary boy who loses as often as he wrestles.

    a) Stooge
    b) Stoolie
    c) Jobber
    d) Hawker

151. Sam Houston hails from

    a) Houston, Texas
    b) Waco, Texas
    c) Dallas, Texas
    d) Staten Island, New York

152. During a promotional appearance, this grappler unknowingly injured a talk show host while attempting to demonstrate a hold. Who was he?

    a) Jerry Lawler
    b) Hulk Hogan
    c) Dr. D
    d) John Studd

153. Identify the television personality.

    a) Andy Kaufman
    b) Richard Belzer
    c) Merv Griffin
    d) Johnny Carson

154. The "hands of stone" belong to

    a) Roberto Ramos
    b) Ronnie Garvin
    c) Jerry Lawler
    d) Rip Rogers

155. ..... makes an appearance in *The Princess Bride*.

    a) Hulk Hogan
    b) Dusty Rhodes
    c) Andre the Giant
    d) John Studd

156. ..... worked in the WWF during the early sixties as Roy Diamond.

    a) The Sheik
    b) Nick Bockwinkel
    c) George Steele
    d) Dusty Rhodes

157. Ricky Steamboat runs an athletic club. What is it called?

    a) Ricky's Gym
    b) Steamboat's Gym
    c) Rick Steamboat's Mid-Atlantic Gym
    d) Rick Steamboat's Gym

158. ..... has been referred to as the poor man's Hulkamania.

    a) Wrestlemania
    b) Machomania
    c) Flairmania
    d) Grapplemania

159. Who was awarded a 1987 Slammy Award as Manager of the Year?

    a) Bobby Heenan
    b) Slick
    c) Jimmy Hart
    d) None of the above

160. Hulk Hogan was once managed by Freddie Blassie.

    True or False?

#163: Superstar Graham's recent comeback was hampered by a severe ..... injury. (Photo by Theo Ehret)

161. Which of the following has little or no ring experience?

    a) Gorilla Monsoon
    b) Gene Okerlund
    c) Lord Alfred Hayes
    d) Fritz Von Erich

162. What was David Von Erich's theme song?

    a) "The Yellow Rose of Texas"
    b) "Texas When I Die"
    c) "Old Man River"
    d) "My Way"

163. Superstar Graham's recent comeback was hampered by a severe ..... injury.

    a) Neck
    b) Back
    c) Hip
    d) Leg

164. This grappler was never on the team.

    a) Larry Latham
    b) The Honky Tonk Man
    c) Jake Roberts
    d) Moondog Spot

165. ..... played for the St. Louis Cardinals as a catcher in their minor league farm system.

    a) Steve Williams
    b) Rick Rude
    c) Randy Savage
    d) Lex Lugar

166. WWF champ Hulk Hogan is a classic

    a) Mark
    b) Broadway
    c) Baby face
    d) Heel

167. General Skandor Akbur and ..... have much in common.

    a) The Legion of Doom
    b) The House of Hell
    c) Devastation Inc.
    d) The Legion of Dishonor

168. When did Ivan Koloff win the WWF heavyweight title?

    a) 1961
    b) 1971
    c) 1981
    d) 1975

169. Whom did he dethrone?

    a) Superstar Graham
    b) Bob Backlund
    c) Buddy Rogers
    d) Bruno Sammartino

170. Select the perfect "mouthpiece."

    a) Slick
    b) Vince McMahon
    c) Gorilla Monsoon
    d) Gene Okerlund

171. Hulk Hogan and Dusty Rhodes are approximately the same weight.

     True or False?

172. ..... runs a professional grappling school at Passariello's Quest Gym.

     a) Killer Kowalski
     b) Bob Orton, Sr.
     c) David Shultz
     d) Ricky Steamboat

173. "Every man has his price" is whose philosophy?

     a) Dusty Rhodes
     b) Ted DiBiase
     c) Slick
     d) Roddy Piper

174. Brady Boone and ..... are cousins.

     a) Billy Jack Haynes
     b) Jerry Lawler
     c) Rick Steiner
     d) Steve Cox

175. The Golden Boy.

     a) Hulk Hogan
     b) Sam Houston
     c) Danny Spivey
     d) Buddy Rose

176. Identify the odd man.

    a) Sam Houston
    b) Bubba Rogers
    c) Ron Simmons
    d) Scott Casey

177. This grappler's truly electric.

    a) Buzz Sawyer
    b) Steve Regal
    c) Buddy Rose
    d) Lex Lugar

178. Who bills himself as the "New Living Legend"?

    a) Larry Zbyszko
    b) Stan Hansen
    c) Buddy Rose
    d) Randy Savage

179. Where does Hulk Hogan call home?

    a) Muscle Beach, California
    b) Venice Beach, California
    c) Tampa, Florida
    d) New Orleans, Louisiana

180. Bobby Heenan, Freddie Blassie, The Grand Wizard, and Lou Albano were all wrestlers at some point in their careers.

    True or False?

181. ..... went under the guise of Big Machine.

    a) Blackjack Mulligan
    b) Andre the Giant
    c) John Studd
    d) Ray Stevens

182. CCC are the initials of what famous mat star?

    a) Carl Creature Carson
    b) Carlos Carlio Coloni
    c) Carlitos Carlos Colon
    d) Carol Carlsoni Colon

183. Randy Savage once played minor league football.

    True or False?

184. Identify the Columbia motion picture which starred Dudley Moore and several top grapplers.

    a) *Paradise Alley*
    b) *Time After Time*
    c) *She Bop*
    d) *Micki & Maude*

185. What wrestlers were highlighted?

    a) Studd, Andre, Hogan
    b) Studd, Andre, Strongbow
    c) Andre, Hogan, Funk
    d) Funk, Andre, Rhodes

186. The Dynamite Kid.

    a) Jimmy Smith
    b) Larry Matthews
    c) Tommy Billington
    d) Eddie Ayers

187. A USMC tattoo adorns his shoulder.

    a) Dusty Rhodes
    b) Blackjack Mulligan
    c) Billy Graham
    d) Sergeant Slaughter

188. Who held two junior heavyweight titles simultaneously?

    a) Barry Alto
    b) Rick Martel
    c) Tiger Mask
    d) Mr. Fuji

189. What exactly is an Ed Moretti?

    a) A Road Warrior
    b) A Moondog
    c) A Sheepherder
    d) A Blackjack

190. Rowdy Roddy Piper was a heavyweight Golden Gloves champion.

    True or False?

#193: Harley Race is a nine-time NWA heavyweight champion. True or False? (Photo by Theo Ehret)

191. How are Iron Mike and Ben Sharpe related?

    a) They are brothers
    b) They are father and son
    c) They are uncle and nephew
    d) They are cousins

192. Jerry Lawler's ..... hospitalized a well-known comic.

    a) Pile-driver
    b) Body-slam
    c) Choke hold
    d) Flying tackle

193. Harley Race is a nine-time NWA heavyweight champion.

    True or False?

194. Ninety minutes of barbarism.

    a) "Blood Match"
    b) "Vampire Grappling"
    c) "Blood To Go"
    d) "Blood Bath"

195. What major event took place at Madison Square Garden on January 23, 1984?

    a) Bruno Sammartino came out of retirement
    b) Hulk Hogan won the WWF title
    c) Bob Backlund lost the WWF title
    d) Hulk Hogan defeated Andre the Giant

196. Someone with little or no inside knowledge of pro wrestling is known as a "mark."

    True or False?

197. ..... is a veteran wrestling analyst.

    a) Steve Basset
    b) Jesse Ventura
    c) Gordon Solie
    d) Al Hayes

198. Colonel DeBeers and ..... are one and the same.

    a) The Polish Prince
    b) King Cobra
    c) Dr. Death
    d) The Crusher

199. Who broke Hillbilly Jim's leg?

    a) John Studd
    b) Rip Rogers
    c) Brutus Beefcake
    d) Jerry Lawler

200. What is Andre the Giant's shoe size?

    a) 16
    b) 22
    c) 26
    d) 19

Heroes and Villains
the answers

1. d—Thunderlips
2. c—Virgil Runnels
3. False
4. d—Miguel Alonzo
5. d—Larry Sharpe
6. c—King Kong Bundy
7. b—A woman wrestler
8. a—Adrian Street
9. c—Andre the Giant
10. b—Brutus Beefcake
11. c—Chris Canyon
12. c—Gene LeBell
13. False
14. c—WBA
15. c—Bam Bam Bigelow
16. a—Bruno Sammartino
17. True
18. c—Liberace
19. c—Bob Orton
20. a—Curt Hennig (Tommy Hennig)
21. a—Wayne Ferris
22. c—Steve Williams
23. c—Tiger Taguchi & Kim Duk
24. True
25. a—Mil Mascaras
26. d—1972
27. a—Joe Frazier
28. a—Ric Flair
29. d—Verne Gagne
30. a—Randy Savage
31. a—Bob and Scott
32. True
33. c—King Parsons
34. a—The Iron Sheik
35. c—3 weeks
36. a—His uncle
37. c—Killer Karl Krupp
38. c—Andy Kaufman
39. c—Mike
40. False
41. a—King Kong Bundy
42. b—Rick Rude
43. a—Stocking
44. b—WWF
45. c—Dos Caras
46. b—Johnny Valentine
47. b—Paul Orndorff
48. c—Sir Oliver Humperdink
49. True
50. b—Andre the Giant
51. c—Colonel DeBeers
52. b—Andre the Giant
53. b—WWF
54. c—Terry Gordy
55. a—Larry Sharpe
56. a—Lillian Ellison
57. c—Window wrap
58. b—Las Vegas
59. b—Lou Albano
60. d—The Sudan
61. b—Ron Bass' whip
62. True
63. b—Jim Crockett Promotions
64. c—Terry Allen
65. a—Wayne Bridges & Otto Wanz
66. True
67. a—Antonio Inoki
68. True
69. d—Scott LeDoux
70. c—The Atlantic City Avalanche
71. c—The Oklahoma Stampede
72. c—Bob Backlund
73. b—NWA
74. d—Giant
75. c—Rick Steiner—Vero Beach, Fl
76. False
77. b—*Grappling News*
78. b—Chris Adams
79. a—268 pounds
80. False
81. c—Bob Backlund
82. b—Bob
83. c—Blood
84. c—Lou Albano
85. d—Vince McMahon, Sr.
86. c—Stu Hart
87. c—itBody Slamro
88. b—24
89. c—Shtick
90. b—Grenoble
91. b—Jack Tunney
92. d—Residences
93. a—Bubba Rogers: 348 pounds, Hendersonville, TN
94. c—Adrian Adonis
95. False
96. a—Hulk Hogan
97. c—New York, Chicago, Los Angeles
98. c— Ricky Steamboat
99. b—Titan Sports
100. d—Draw

101. c—David Schultz
102. b—John Stossel
103. b—Is wrestling fake?
104. a—WWWF
105. b—Vinnie Valentino
106. c—Ivan Putski
107. True
108. a—The Funks
109. c—Junkyard Dog
110. b—Ted DiBiase
111. c—Dusty Rhodes
112. c—Bill Apter
113. c—Randy Savage
114. b—Austin Idol
115. a—Guitar
116. c—Iron Mike DiBiase
117. d—The Crusher
118. c—The Liberty Wrestling Alliance
119. a—They are hillbillies
120. c—1974
121. c—Jerry & Terry Lawler
122. d—Bill Eadie
123. d—The War To Settle The Score
124. b—He married Wendi Richter
125. False
126. c—King Kong Bundy, S.D. Jones
127. b—Sergeant Slaughter
128. a—Helen Hild
129. c—Outback Jack
130. b—Hockey
131. c—Buddy Rogers, Ric Flair
132. b—Studd wins 20-man battle royal
133. a—George Steele
134. b—Plant
135. c—Terry Funk
136. d—Sylvester Ritter
137. d—John Boyer
138. d—Crusher Blackwell
139. False
140. a—Jerry Lawler
141. d—Vladimir Pietrov
142. d—Billy Graham & Tully Blanchard
143. c—93,000
144. c—Pontiac Silverdome
145. a—Pedro Morales
146. d—Catch-as-catch-can
147. d—Kendo Nagazaki
148. c—Ron Bass
149. a—Linda Kelly
150. c—Jobber
151. b—Waco, Texas
152. b—Hulk Hogan
153. b—Richard Belzer
154. b—Ronnie Garvin
155. c—Andre the Giant
156. b—Nick Bockwinkel
157. c—Rick Stemaboat's Mid-Atlantic Gym
158. b—Machomania
159. d—None of the above
160. True
161. b—Gene Okerlund
162. b—"Texas When I Die"
163. c—Hip
164. c—Jake Roberts
165. c—Randy Savage
166. c—Baby face
167. c—Devastation Inc.
168. b—1971
169. d—Bruno Sammartino
170. a—Slick
171. True
172. c—David Shultz
173. b—Ted DiBiase
174. a—Billy Jack Haynes
175. c—Danny Spivey
176. c—Ron Simmons
177. b—Steve Regal
178. a—Larry Zbyszko
179. b—Venice Beach, California
180. False
181. a—Blackjack Mulligan
182. c—Carlitos Carlos Colon
183. False
184. d—*Micki & Maude*
185. b—Studd, Andre, Strongbow
186. c—Tommy Billington
187. b—Blackjack Mulligan
188. c—Tiger Mask
189. b—A Moondog
190. False
191. c—They are uncle and nephew
192. a—Pile-driver
193. False
194. d—"Blood Bath"
195. b—Hulk Hogan won the WWF title
196. True
197. c—Gordon Solie
198. a—The Polish Prince
199. c—Brutus Beefcake
200. b—22

PART II
Tag Teams

Tag Teams

1. ..... and Tama perform as the dynamic Islanders.

   a) Hama
   b) Taku
   c) Haku
   d) Kama

2. Randy "Macho Man" Savage and Lanny Poffo once teamed up as The Poffo Brothers.

   True or False?

3. Ken Patera, Jerry Blackwell and manager Sheik Adnann El-Kaissey were known as

   a) The Sheiks
   b) The Middle East Connection
   c) The Egyptians
   d) The Middle East Assassins

4. Hulk Hogan's tag team partners have included all of the following except

   a) Hillbilly Jim
   b) Mr. T
   c) Kevin Von Erich
   d) Iron Mike Sharpe

5. The Road Warriors tip the scales at

   a) 567 pounds
   b) 662 pounds
   c) 521 pounds
   d) 630 pounds

6. Paul Ellering's nickname is

   a) Precious
   b) Prince
   c) Precocious
   d) Petty

7. Mr. Fuji's Demolition.

   a) Hawk and Ax
   b) Smash and Bash
   c) Ax and Smash
   d) Shake and Bake

8. Roy Heffernan was once a member of this great combo. What was it called?

   a) The Mongols
   b) The Fabulous Kangaroos
   c) The Spoilers
   d) The Cattlemen

9. We knew the Nelson Brothers as

   a) Art Nelson & Stan Nelson
   b) Stan Wright & Art Nelson
   c) Art Nelson & Stan Holek
   d) Mike Nelson & Art Nelson

10. During what wrestling extravaganza did the British Bulldogs win their initial WWF tag team title?

   a) Jim Crockett Sr. Memorial Cup
   b) "Saturday Night's Main Event"
   c) Wrestlemania II
   d) The Great American Bash

11. Joe Namath and Phil Esposito have recently signed an exclusive contract to wrestle for Vince McMahon as a masked duo.

    True of False?

12. ..... guided the Galaxians.

    a) Lou Albano
    b) Jim Cornette
    c) Sonny King
    d) The Grand Wizard

13. An interracial partnership.

    a) Rocky King & Tony Atlas
    b) Bubba Rogers & Chance McQuade
    c) The Blackjacks
    d) Rocky King & Chance McQuade

14. The song "Born in the U.S.A." was most closely associated with what tag team?

    a) The Road Warriors
    b) Rick Morton & Robert Gibson
    c) Barry Windham & Mike Rotundo
    d) The Freebirds

15. Who does Bobby Heenan refer to as "La Bomba" and "Lucky Pierre"?

    a) Tito Santana & Frenchie Martin
    b) Tito Santana & Rick Martel
    c) Hercules Hernandez & Rick Martel
    d) Johnny Rodz & Frenchie Martin

16. Identify the Midnight Rockers.

    a) Sean Michaels & Marty Jannetty
    b) Mark Anthony & Johnny Wilhoyt
    c) Mark Batten & Johnny Wilhoyt
    d) Sean Michaels & Johnny Wilhoyt

17. The late ..... will be best remembered as the tag team partner of his brother, Wild Bill.

    a) Russ Sawyer
    b) Frank Gagne
    c) Scott Irwin
    d) Gary Valentine

18. ..... serves as manager of The Sheepherders.

    a) Lou Albano
    b) Paul Ellering
    c) Jonathan Boyd
    d) Jimmy Hart

19. Chief Jay Strongbow and ..... held the WWF team belt in 1972.

    a) Jules Strongbow
    b) Sonny King
    c) Chief Billy White Wolf
    d) Ted Oates

20. Which of the following is a fictitious team?

    a) The Enforcers
    b) The Gladiators
    c) The Faggots
    d) The Mod Squad

#24: Ernie Ladd was an original member of The Harlem Express. True or False? (Photo by Theo Ehret)

21. Greg Gagne and Jim Brunzell formed a partnership known as

    a) The Masked Marvels
    b) The High Rollers
    c) The High Flyers
    d) The Mighty Mights

22. One-half of a Bolshevik equals

    a) Nikolai Volkoff
    b) Dusty Rhodes
    c) The Kremlin Kid
    d) Nikita Koloff

23. ..... are the Blackjacks.

    a) Mulligan Sr. & Roberts
    b) Rhodes & Lanza
    c) Morton & Lanza
    d) Mulligan Sr. & Lanza

24. Ernie Ladd was an original member of The Harlem Express.

    True or False?

25. ..... created The Legion of Doom.

    a) Lou Albano
    b) Paul Ellering
    c) Ernie Roth
    d) Jim Holiday

26. Two members of this group have included

    a) The Spoilers & Kamala
    b) The Spoilers & Jake Roberts
    c) Ivan Koloff & The Grapplers
    d) Ivan Koloff & Steve Keirn

27. New Zealand is the home of

    a) The Midnight Express
    b) The Down Under Boys
    c) The Sheepherders
    d) The Road Warriors

28. Jonathan Boyd and Luke Williams are really

    a) Brothers
    b) Cousins
    c) Father & son
    d) Uncle & nephew

29. The Road Warriors have made guest appearances on *The A-Team*, *Miami Vice*, and *Remington Steele*.

    True or False?

30. Identify the Hollywood Blondes.

    a) Wendi Richter & Susan Starr
    b) Mad Maxine & Susan Starr
    c) Rip Rogers & Ted Oates
    d) Tommy Rogers & Robert Gibson

31. ..... was once Paul Ellering's tag team partner.

    a) Lou Albano
    b) Steve Olsonoski
    c) Michael Hayes
    d) Butch Miller

32. The Blackjacks were handled by Bobby Heenan.

    True or False?

33. Bob Orton and his dad were never teamed.

    True or False?

34. ..... were Lou Albano's initial tag team champions.

    a) The Mongols
    b) The Valiants
    c) The Samoans
    d) The Moondogs

35. Albano himself was once a member of

    a) The Godfathers
    b) The Italians
    c) The Sicilians
    d) The Pizza Connection

36. Who was his partner?

    a) Tony Galento
    b) Tony Altamore
    c) Tony Baggi
    d) Frankie Martino

37. ..... was known as "The Third Samoan."

    a) Ali
    b) Jimmy
    c) Sammy
    d) Freddie

38. How old was he upon joining the group?

    a) 24
    b) 19
    c) 16
    d) 29

39. ..... is Davey Boy Smith's talented tag mate.

    a) The Hot Dog Kid
    b) TNT
    c) The Dynamic Kid
    d) The Dynamite Kid

40. ..... is a Lover Boy.

    a) Norvell Austin
    b) Dennis Condrey
    c) Randy Rose
    d) Rick Morton

41. The Midnight Express is one of the few gay combos in pro wrestling today.

    True or False?

42. Hector and ..... are related.

    a) Chico
    b) Chavo
    c) Jimmy
    d) Jose

43. Barry Windham and Mike Rotundo entered the WWF under the tutelage of

    a) Freddie Blassie
    b) The Grand Wizard
    c) Lou Albano
    d) Paul Ellering

44. They defeated Adrian Adonis and ..... for the tag team belt.

    a) Dick Murdoch
    b) Bret Hart
    c) Ken Patera
    d) Tony Atlas

45. Jim Neidhart married Bret Hart's ..... and became "family."

    a) Mother
    b) Niece
    c) Sister
    d) Cousin

46. How would one best describe Mr. Miller of the Sheepherders?

    a) Crazy
    b) Wild
    c) Insane
    d) Killer

47. Paul Roma and Jim Powers throw their weight around as

    a) The Young Sicilians
    b) The Young Samoans
    c) The Young Stallions
    d) The Young Italians

48. Jim Powers is a Brooklyn boy.

    True or False?

49. Which of the following partnerships never existed?

    a) Jimmy & Johnny Valiant
    b) Greg Gagne & Jim Brunzell
    c) Nick Bockwinkel & Ray Stevens
    d) Ole Anderson & Ricky Steamboat

50. Jerry Brisco, one-half of the renowned Brisco Brothers, has held the NWA junior heavyweight title.

    True or False?

51. Stan Lane and Bobby Eaton have been tag mates of Koko B. Ware.

    True or False?

52. Bobby Eaton is known in wrestling circles as

    a) Bad
    b) Beautiful
    c) Nasty
    d) Gorgeous

53. What team has more difficulty getting around the ring?

    a) Strike Force
    b) The British Bulldogs
    c) The Rock 'n' Roll Express
    d) Hulk Hogan & Mr. T

54. What individual has guided the greatest number of teams to championships?

    a) Lou Albano
    b) Freddie Blassie
    c) Jimmy Hart
    d) The Grand Wizard

55. Sergeant Slaughter and ..... were a highly successful combo in the NWA.

    a) Don Kernodle
    b) Jerry Lawler
    c) Dusty Rhodes
    d) Lanny Poffo

56. Chief Jay Strongbow and ..... held the WWF team title in 1977.

    a) Jules Strongbow
    b) Chief Billy White Wolf
    c) Sonny King
    d) Chief Billy White Dog

57. The WWF's Islanders are put through their paces by

    a) Slick
    b) Jimmy Hart
    c) Paul Ellering
    d) Bobby Heenan

58. Who succeeded Freddie Blassie as manager of The Iron Sheik and Nikolai Volkoff?

    a) Lou Albano
    b) Slick
    c) Paul Ellering
    d) Jimmy Hart

59. Rick Martel and ..... flex their muscles as Strike Force.

    a) Bret Hart
    b) Lex Lugar
    c) Tito Santana
    d) Tony Atlas

60. Rick Morton belongs to the popular

    a) Rock 'n' Roll Express
    b) Midnight Express
    c) Fabulous Ones
    d) Flying Fondas

61. Identify Rick's tag mate.

    a) Steve Keirn
    b) Butch Miller
    c) Robert Gibson
    d) Tommy Rogers

62. What two black grapplers have worn the WWF tag team belt?

    a) Tony Atlas & Junkyard Dog
    b) Junkyard Dog & Sonny King
    c) Tony Atlas & Sonny King
    d) Tony Atlas & Rocky Johnson

63. Nikita Koloff and ..... call themselves The Superpowers.

    a) The Iron Sheik
    b) Dusty Rhodes
    c) Bubba Rogers
    d) Sergeant Slaughter

64. Barry Windham has tagged with younger brother Kendall.

    True or False?

65. Prior to joining the Fabulous Ones, Stan Lane and ..... teamed up to capture the Florida State combo championship.

    a) Bryan St. John
    b) Billy St. James
    c) Rocky Johnson
    d) Richie Watson

66. The Fabulous Freebirds hailed from

   a) Backstreet, U.S.A.
   b) Main Street, U.S.A.
   c) Big D
   d) Bad Street, U.S.A.

67. Mike Rotundo and Barry Windham are brothers.

   True or False?

68. Which of the following is out of place?

   a) Koko B. Ware
   b) Butch Reed
   c) Bubba Rogers
   d) Kamala

69. ..... and Jay are the Strongbows.

   a) Jules
   b) Barry
   c) Mark
   d) Jack

70. Remember ..... and ..... as the Dirty White Boys?

   a) Len Anthony & Tony Denton
   b) Rick Morton & Mike Stone
   c) Len Denton & Tony Anthony
   d) Bob Orton Jr. & Killer Brooks

#75: Female combos are the most popular form of team competition. True or False? (Photo by Theo Ehret)

71. All of the following have been members of the Midnight Express except

    a) Dennis Condrey
    b) Norvell Austin
    c) Randy Rose
    d) Buddy Rose

72. The Samoans were handled by ..... for most of their career.

    a) The Grand Wizard
    b) Freddie Blassie
    c) Lou Albano
    d) Paul Ellering

73. Koko B. Ware and Norvell Austin claimed membership in

    a) The Dirty Black Boys
    b) The Pretty Young Things
    c) The Uptown Boys
    d) The Harlem Express

74. Who gave spirit to The New Generation?

    a) Mr. Fuji
    b) Jimmy Hart
    c) Paul Ellering
    d) Tojo Yamamoto

75. Female combos are the most popular form of team competition.

    True or False?

76. Identify the two "superstars" of pro grappling.

    a) Graham & Snuka
    b) Roberts & Rhodes
    c) Graham & Dundee
    d) Rhodes & Flair

77. The Four Horsemen have included all of the following except

    a) Tully Blanchard
    b) Ric Flair
    c) Jerry Lawler
    d) Lex Lugar

78. Ric Flair and The One Man Gang were tag partners.

    True or False?

79. ..... was responsible for the initial success of the Fabulous Ones.

    a) Jackie Fargo
    b) Ernie Roth
    c) Lou Albano
    d) Jimmy Hart

80. Ronnie Garvin hooked up with ..... to create the Risky Business Boys.

    a) Dusty Rhodes
    b) Steve Regal
    c) Rick Morton
    d) Scott Hall

81. Hector and Chavo Guerrero wore the WWF team crown briefly during the early seventies.

    True or False?

82. Jack Brisco was NWA heavyweight champion at one point in his career.

    True or False?

83. ..... and Hawk are The Road Warriors.

    a) Killer
    b) Hogg
    c) Butcher
    d) Animal

84. The UWF championship belt has been worn by

    a) Arn Anderson & Scott Hall
    b) Dusty Rhodes & Matt Borne
    c) Buzz Sawyer & Matt Borne
    d) John Tatum & Jack Victory

85. Luke Williams' nickname is

    a) Crazy
    b) Wild One
    c) Killer
    d) The Man

86. ..... did his thing with the Bruise Brothers.

    a) Lou Albano
    b) Jimmy Hart
    c) Jim Holiday
    d) Paul Ellering

87. They were card-carrying members of "The American Express."

    a) Junkyard Dog & Tony Atlas
    b) Brad Jones & Tony Atlas
    c) Barry Windham & Mike Rotundo
    d) Ricky Morton & Koko B. Ware

88. These two men are truly fantastic.

    a) Tommy Hodges & Bobby Fulton
    b) Jimmy Hart & Bobby Foster
    c) Tommy Rogers & Bobby Fulton
    d) Koko B. Ware & Rocky Johnson

89. The Pretty Young Things were managed by

    a) Tommy Rogers
    b) Percy Pringle
    c) Bobby Heenan
    d) Koko B. Ware

90. Raymond and ..... comprise the Rougeau Brothers.

    a) Frenchie
    b) Jacques
    c) Andre
    d) Anton

91. ..... brought the Zambui Express together.

    a) Lou Albano
    b) Bobby Heenan
    c) Kevin Sullivan
    d) Graham Michaels

92. Mr. Fuji and Tiger Chung Lee formed a team partnership known as

    a) The Orient Express
    b) The Oriental Connection
    c) The Orient Slayers
    d) The Oriental Brothers

93. The Masked Medics were never a grappling duo.

    True or False?

94. The British Bulldogs had ..... as their mascot.

    a) Mattie
    b) Elizabeth
    c) Maggie
    d) Matilda

95. Who were Pork Chop and the Dream Machine?

    a) Jerry Blackwell & Dusty Rhodes
    b) The Uptown Boys
    c) The Grapplers
    d) The Bruise Brothers

96. The Maniac and ..... are one and the same.

    a) Paul Ellering
    b) Jonathan Boyd
    c) Luke Williams
    d) Rip Rogers

97. ..... were an updated version of the Fabulous Kangaroos.

    a) Don Kent & Johnny Heffernan
    b) Don Kent & Roy Heffernan
    c) Roy & Johnny Heffernan
    d) Roy Heffernan & Robert Morton

98. What grapplers made up the Zambui Express?

    a) Elija Akeem & Kareem Muhammad
    b) Elija Akeem & Kamala
    c) Rocky Johnson & Tony Atlas
    d) Abdullah the Butcher & Kareen Muhammad

99. Lou Albano has managed all of the following to championships except

    a) The Moondogs
    b) The Samoans
    c) The Yukon Lumberjacks
    d) The Midnight Express

100. Who were the original Samoans?

    a) Afa & Jimmy
    b) Jimmy & Ali
    c) Afa & Sika
    d) Sika & Sammy

Tag Teams
the answers

1. c—Haku
2. True
3. a—The Sheiks
4. c—Kevin Von Erich
5. a—567 pounds
6. a—Precious
7. c—Ax and Smash
8. b—The Fabulous Kangaroos
9. c—Art Nelson & Stan Holek
10. c—Wrestemania II
11. False
12. b—Jim Cornette
13. d—Rocky King & Chance McQuade
14. c—Barry Windham & Mike Rotundo
15. b—Tito Santana & Rick Martel
16. a—Sean Michaels & Marty Jannetty
17. c—Scott Irwin
18. c—Jonathan Boyd
19. b—Sonny King
20. c—The Faggots
21. c—The High Flyers
22. a—Nikolai Volkoff
23. d—Mulligan Sr. & Lanza
24. False
25. b—Paul Ellering
26. b—The Spoiler & Jake Roberts
27. c—The Sheepherders
28. b—Cousins
29. False
30. c—Rip Rogers & Ted Oates
31. b—Steve Olsonoski
32. True
33. False
34. a—The Mongols
35. c—The Sicilians
36. b—Tony Altamore
37. c—Sammy
38. b—19
39. d—The Dynamite Kid
40. b—Dennis Condrey
41. False
42. b—Chavo
43. c—Lou Albano
44. a—Dick Murdoch
45. c—Sister
46. b—Wild
47. c—The Young Stallions
48. True
49. d—Ole Anderson & Ricky Steamboat
50. True
51. True
52. b—Beautiful
53. d—Hulk Hogan & Mr. T
54. a—Lou Albano
55. a—Don Kernodle
56. b—Chief Billy White Wolf
57. d—Bobby Heenan
58. b—Slick
59. c—Tito Santana
60. a—Rock 'n' Roll Express
61. c—Robert Gibson
62. d—Tony Atlas & Rocky Johnson
63. b—Dusty Rhodes
64. True
65. a—Bryan St. John
66. d—Bad Street, U.S.A.
67. False
68. c—Bubba Rogers
69. a—Jules
70. c—Len Denton & Tony Anthony
71. d—Buddy Rose
72. c—Lou Albano
73. b—The Pretty Young Things
74. d—Tojo Yamamoto
75. False
76. c—Graham & Dundee
77. c—Jerry Lawler
78. False
79. a—Jackie Fargo
80. a—Dusty Rhodes
81. False
82. True
83. d—Animal
84. d—John Tatum & Jack Victory
85. a—Crazy
86. b—Jimmy Hart
87. c—Barry Windham & Mike Rotundo
88. c—Tommy Rogers & Bobby Fulton
89. b—Percy Pringle
90. b—Jacques
91. c—Kevin Sullivan
92. b—The Oriental Connection
93. False
94. d—Matilda
95. d—The Bruise Brothers
96. b—Jonathan Boyd
97. a—Don Kent & Johnny Heffernan
98. a—Elija Akeem & Kareem Muhammad
99. d—The Midnight Express
100. c—Afa & Sika

PART III
Legends
of the Past

Legends of the Past

1. In what film did Gorgeous George appear?

   a) *The Gorgeous George Story*
   b) *Alias Jesse James*
   c) *Alias the Champ*
   d) *The Perfumed Dandy*

2. The foremost figure in the rise of professional wrestling was

   a) Rube Wright
   b) Frank Gotch
   c) Tom Gorman
   d) Stan Holek

3. Danny Plechas and ..... are synonymous.

   a) Bullfrog
   b) Homer
   c) Bulldog
   d) Deadman

4. ''The Terrible Teuton'' could only be

   a) Vincent Von Ryan
   b) Waldo Von Erich
   c) Killer Kowalski
   d) Ed Lewis

5. Barefoot wrestling achieved popularity during the reign of

   a) Ed Lewis
   b) Bruno Sammartino
   c) Antonino Rocca
   d) Butch Lewis

6. El Santo was a masked wrestler.

   True or False?

7. The skull butt was popularized by

   a) Skull Sheldon
   b) Bobo Brazil
   c) Skull Murphy
   d) Bob Orton Sr.

8. Who held the NWA title in 1952?

   a) Verne Gagne
   b) Lou Thesz
   c) Freddie Blassie
   d) Antonino Rocca

9. Who was Ernie Roth?

   a) A wrestler
   b) A manager
   c) An announcer
   d) A promoter

10. Abdullah Farouk was the manager of

   a) The Iron Sheik
   b) Abdullah the Butcher
   c) The Sheik
   d) Armstrong Kay

11. What university did Joe Pazanka attend?

   a) University of Maryland
   b) New York University
   c) University of Minnesota
   d) Harvard University

12. The birthplace of Antonino Rocca was said to be

   a) Argentina
   b) Italy
   c) New York City
   d) Puerto Rico

13. This grappler once floored Joe Louis in a heavyweight boxing match. Who was he?

   a) Ed Lewis
   b) Tony Galento
   c) Man Mountain Dean
   d) Rube Wright

14. ..... was Joe Pazanka's favorite tag team partner.

   a) Mr. Fuji
   b) Mr. Moto
   c) Mr. Tokyo Rose
   d) Freddie Blassie

15. ..... was known as "The Champ."

   a) Tony Galento
   b) Joe Pazanka
   c) Bruno Sammartino
   d) Art Nelson

#18: The ..... was an Antonino Rocca trademark. (Photo by Gene Gordon)

16. Famed Minneapolis promoter Tony Stecher was very instru-
mental in the early career of

   a) Earl McCready
   b) Joe Pazanka
   c) Bill Wright
   d) Lou Thesz

17. What was Tony Galento's nickname?

   a) Mountain
   b) Haystacks
   c) Two Ton
   d) Big Tony

18. The ..... was an Antonino Rocca trademark.

   a) Claw hold
   b) Head butt
   c) Flying dropkick
   d) Neck lock

19. J. Wellington Radcliff was really

   a) Lou Albano
   b) Ernie Roth
   c) Handsome Johnny Barend
   d) Blackjack Maurice

20. This well-known wrestler and boxer appeared in several the-
atrical productions, including *Guys and Dolls*. Who was he?

   a) Man Mountain Dean
   b) Tony Galento
   c) Bruno Sammartino
   d) Handsome Johnny Barend

21. Han Schmidt represented what nation?

    a) Germany
    b) Austria
    c) England
    d) Canada

22. ..... held the NWA title six times.

    a) Killer Kowalski
    b) Lou Thesz
    c) Buddy Rogers
    d) The Iron Sheik

23. What is Killer Kowalski's first name?

    a) Waldo
    b) Nicholas
    c) Wladek
    d) David

24. Killer Kowalski runs a school for aspiring wrestlers. Where is it located?

    a) Boston
    b) Detroit
    c) North Carolina
    d) Los Angeles

25. Whose ear did Kowalski sever during a match in the early fifties?

    a) Otto Wagner
    b) Pedro Morales
    c) Yukon Eric
    d) Johnny Barend

26. Who was the heaviest wrestler in pro history?

   a) Haystacks Calhoun
   b) Happy Humphrey
   c) Andre the Giant
   d) Man Mountain Dean

27. The nickname "Riot Call" belongs to

   a) Jim Wright
   b) Freddie Blassie
   c) Joe Baker
   d) Antonino Rocca

28. ..... has never held the WWF heavyweight title.

   a) Pedro Morales
   b) Ivan Koloff
   c) Buddy Rose
   d) The Iron Sheik

29. "Nature Boy" referred to whom?

   a) Buddy Roberts
   b) Ed Lewis
   c) Buddy Rogers
   d) Lou Thesz

30. ..... left the "squared circle" to become an evangelist.

   a) Paul Bunyan
   b) Ed Lewis
   c) Jim Wright
   d) Rube Wright

31. Who was the first WWF heavyweight champion?

    a) Bruno Sammartino
    b) Buddy Rogers
    c) Pedro Morales
    d) Antonino Rocca

32. Where was Earl McCready born?

    a) Newfoundland
    b) Toronto
    c) Lansdowne, Ontario
    d) Ottawa

33. ..... was named Mexico's most popular grappler of all-time.

    a) Pedro Morales
    b) Jose Santana
    c) El Santo
    d) El Ramos

34. ..... went by the nickname "The Strangler."

    a) Stan Holek
    b) Jim Wright
    c) Ed Lewis
    d) Bob Orton Sr.

35. The term "Living Legend" is associated with what classic star?

    a) Buddy Rogers
    b) Killer Kowalski
    c) Bruno Sammartino
    d) Billy Graham

36. Everyone knew Bill Watson as

    a) Sweet William
    b) Whipper
    c) The Man
    d) The Whaler

37. On October 27, 1953 this wrestler won his 152nd consecutive bout in the United States. Who was he?

    a) Antonino Rocca
    b) Yukon Eric
    c) Raphael Halperin
    d) Han Schmidt

38. Who was Robert Friedrich?

    a) Yukon Eric
    b) Bill Watson
    c) Ed Lewis
    d) Earl McCready

39. Which of the following does not belong?

    a) The Grand Wizard
    b) Mr. Kleen
    c) J. Wellington Radcliffe
    d) Master Thomas

40. Who were "the big three" of pro wrestling in 1953?

    a) Sammartino, Rocca, Gagne
    b) Rocca, Gagne, Lewis
    c) Rocca, Gagne, Thesz
    d) Rocca, Gagne, Kowalski

41. In what year did Lou Thesz win his first NWA title?

    a) 1927
    b) 1937
    c) 1947
    d) 1944

42. Whom did he defeat in that match?

    a) Man Mountain Dean
    b) Buddy Rogers
    c) Everett Marshall
    d) Killer Kowalski

43. This great catch-as-catch-can grappler had only one eye. Who was he?

    a) Ed Lewis
    b) Tom Gorman
    c) Tom Jenkins
    d) Baron Leone

44. Lloyd Kelsey employed the deadly

    a) Claw hold
    b) Camel clutch
    c) Bear hug
    d) Cobra hold

45. ..... was the highest paid wrestler in 1952.

    a) Lou Thesz
    b) Yukon Eric
    c) Antonino Rocca
    d) Buddy Rogers

#50: How much did Haystacks Calhoun weigh? (Photo by Gene Gordon)

46. What was Happy Humphrey's real name?

    a) Billy Williams
    b) William Cobb
    c) Billy Larson
    d) William J. Lawson

47. Happy Humphrey was a country boy from

    a) Virginia
    b) Alabama
    c) Georgia
    d) North Carolina

48. What was Frank Gotch's won-loss record?

    a) 154-6
    b) 217-16
    c) 307-26
    d) 97-3

49. ..... once served as a trainer for John L. Sullivan.

    a) Ed Lewis
    b) Man Mountain Dean
    c) Tony Galento
    d) Bill Muldoon

50. How much did Haystacks Calhoun weigh?

    a) 601 pounds
    b) 502 pounds
    c) 802 pounds
    d) 695 pounds

51. What was Antonino Rocca's "secret of life"?

    a) Plenty of sleep
    b) Plenty of sex
    c) No sex
    d) Good blood circulation

52. What was Tony Galento's real name?

    a) Vincent Anthony Galento
    b) Dominick Anthony Galento
    c) Louis Anthony Galento
    d) Vincent Louis Galento

53. Bill Muldoon was once a member of the New York State Athletic Commission.

    True or False?

54. Who defeated Lou Thesz on November 21, 1947 for the NWA title?

    a) Bill Watson
    b) Ed Lewis
    c) Vern Rule
    d) Bill Longson

55. Before entering the world of pro wrestling, Gus Sonnenberg played

    a) Baseball
    b) Football
    c) Basketball
    d) Polo

56. ..... said he would live to the 150 years young.

    a) Jim Wright
    b) Gorgeous George
    c) Skull Murphy
    d) Antonino Rocca

57. What was George Zaharias' true moniker?

    a) Frank Gucci
    b) Victor Vetoyanis
    c) Charles Tetoyanos
    d) Theodore Vetoyanis

58. Who billed himself as "The Hollywood Fashion Plate"?

    a) Gorgeous George
    b) Freddie Blassie
    c) Buddy Rogers
    d) Billy Graham

59. Stan Stasiak enjoyed being called

    a) Killer
    b) The Man
    c) The Vampire
    d) Wolf Man

60. Buddy Rogers once hosted an interview program titled

    a) "Rogers Rangers"
    b) "Rogers Raiders"
    c) "Rogers Corner"
    d) "Buddy's Barn"

#67: Killer Kowalski was known for what maneuver? (Photo by Theo Ehret)

61. Max Palmer was really

    a) Max the Ax
    b) Paul Bunyan
    c) Jay Strongbow
    d) Kenny Watson

62. ..... is the only man in pro wrestling history to regain the WWF heavyweight title.

    a) Buddy Rogers
    b) Pedro Morales
    c) Bruno Sammartino
    d) Superstar Billy Graham

63. What classic performer was known as "The Russian Lion"?

    a) Bruno Sammartino
    b) Man Mountain Dean
    c) George Hackenschmidt
    d) Ralph Von Erich

64. Gorilla Monsoon is legally referred to as

    a) Eddie Mack
    b) Salvatore Burruni
    c) Tony Canzoneri
    d) None of the above

65. Alfred Hodgson and ..... were one and the same.

    a) Jack Reynolds
    b) Jack Wentworth
    c) Bill Watson
    d) Skull Murphy

66. ..... held the NWA title in 1960.

a) Yukon Eric
b) Buddy Rogers
c) Pat O'Connor
d) Killer Kowalski

67. Killer Kowalski was known for what maneuver?

a) Cobra clutch
b) Claw hold
c) Head butt
d) Flying rope

68. The great football player Bronko Nugurski was once a professional wrestler.

True or False?

69. Humboldt, Iowa was the birthplace of

a) Ed Lewis
b) Jim Wright
c) Frank Gotch
d) Rube Wright

70. Dr. Jerry Graham and Roy Heffernan were always rivals.

True or False?

71. Who was the tallest wrestler ever?

    a) Andre the Giant
    b) Paul Bunyan
    c) Hulk Hogan
    d) Haystacks Calhoun

72. How tall was he?

    a) 6' 10"
    b) 7' 2"
    c) 8' 2"
    d) 7' 6"

73. Who dethroned the seemingly invincible Tom Jenkins?

    a) Lou Thesz
    b) Frank Gotch
    c) Bill Wright
    d) Earl McCready

74. What was Gorgeous George's real name?

    a) Joe Baker
    b) Victor Wagner Ross
    c) George Wagner Ross
    d) George Raymond Wagner

75. What grappler has held the WWF heavyweight crown longer than any other man in history?

    a) Buddy Rogers
    b) Hulk Hogan
    c) Bruno Sammartino
    d) Bob Backlund

76. All of the following were champions except

    a) Earl McCready
    b) Freddie Blassie
    c) Armstrong Kay
    d) Bob Orton Sr.

77. How old was Max Palmer when he died?

    a) 82
    b) 32
    c) 56
    d) 76

78. In what year did Jack Wentworth turn pro?

    a) 1922
    b) 1932
    c) 1942
    d) 1939

79. Waldo Von Erich once held the European heavyweight title.

    True or False?

80. This wrestler was quite successful under the name of Lu Kim during the latter part of his career. Most fans knew him as

    a) Jim Wright
    b) Ed Lewis
    c) Rube Wright
    d) Art Nelson

81. ..... defeated Pedro Morales for the WWF heavyweight crown.

    a) Superstar Graham
    b) Bruno Sammartino
    c) Stan Stasiak
    d) Buddy Rogers

82. He worked as a funeral director, mortician and hair stylist outside the ring. The public knew him as

    a) Mr. Kleen
    b) The Mad Greek
    c) King Cobra
    d) Prince Erik

83. In what film did Paul Bunyan appear?

    a) *The Paul Bunyan Story*
    b) *Tarzan*
    c) *Jungle Jim*
    d) *The Killer Ape*

84. What was King Cobra's real name?

    a) Lloyd Kelsey
    b) George Zaharias
    c) Jack Wentworth
    d) Butch Lewis

85. Ed Lewis held the grappling championship between the years

    a) 1919-1935
    b) 1920-1932
    c) 1925-1937
    d) 1935-1947

86. Who finally defeated Lewis to capture the title?

    a) Lou Thesz
    b) Frank Gotch
    c) Gus Sonnenberg
    d) Buddy Rogers

87. In 1963, the WWF created a tournament to establish its initial heavyweight champion. Who were the finalists?

    a) Buddy Rogers & Killer Kowalski
    b) Pedro Morales & Antonino Rocca
    c) Antonino Rocca & Buddy Rogers
    d) Buddy Rogers & Lou Thesz

88. He introduced the flying tackle to professional wrestling. Identify this superb athlete.

    a) Antonino Rocca
    b) Gus Sonnenberg
    c) Freddie Blassie
    d) Stan Holek

89. George Zaharias was nicknamed

    a) The Flying Greek from Cripple Creek
    b) The Crying Greek from Cripple Creek
    c) The Crowing Greek from Ripple Creek
    d) The Mad Greek

90. ..... was Jack Wentworth's hometown.

    a) New York City
    b) England
    c) Canada
    d) Wales

#96: How long did it take Bruno Sammartino to defeat Buddy Rogers for the WWF crown? (Photo by Gene Gordon)

91. ..... held the Midwest title in 1954.

    a) Antonino Rocca
    b) Lou Thesz
    c) Vern Gagne
    d) Buddy Rose

92. Gorgeous George was always a perfumed dandy.

    True or False?

93. ..... was the first noted American professional freestyle champion.

    a) Gus Sonnenberg
    b) Lou Thesz
    c) Vern Gagne
    d) Tom Jenkins

94. Ernie Roth managed all of the following except

    a) Greg Valentine
    b) Bob Backlund
    c) Killer Kowalski
    d) Ray Stevens

95. "The Blonde Canadian" referred to whom?

    a) Pistol Pete Peterson
    b) Pat Patterson
    c) Johnny Barend
    d) Rip Rogers

96. How long did it take Bruno Sammartino to defeat Buddy Rogers for the WWF crown?

    a) 27 seconds
    b) 47 seconds
    c) 57 seconds
    d) 1 minute and 57 seconds

97. "The Champ from St. Louis" was

    a) Ed Lewis
    b) Buddy Rogers
    c) Vern Gagne
    d) Lou Thesz

98. Who was the fifth man to hold the WWF title?

    a) Ivan Koloff
    b) Bob Backlund
    c) Stan Stasiak
    d) Superstar Billy Graham

99. ..... was "The Big O" of professional wrestling.

    a) Bobo Olson
    b) Bob Orton Sr.
    c) Bob Orton Jr.
    d) Oleg of Norway

100. Who could rightfully be called "The Mr. Television of Professional Wrestling"?

    a) Bruno Sammartino
    b) Antonino Rocca
    c) Lou Thesz
    d) Buddy Rogers

Legends of the Past
the answers

1. c—*Alias the Champ*
2. b—Frank Gotch
3. d—Bulldog
4. b—Waldo Von Erich
5. c—Antonino Rocca
6. True
7. c—Skull Murphy
8. b—Lou Thesz
9. b—A manager
10. c—The Sheik
11. c—University of Minnesota
12. b—Italy
13. b—Tony Galento
14. b—Mr. Moto
15. b—Joe Pazanka
16. b—Joe Pazanka
17. c—Two Ton
18. c—Flying dropkick
19. b—Ernie Roth
20. b—Tony Galento
21. a—Germany
22. b—Lou Thesz
23. c—Wladek
24. a—Boston
25. c—Yukon Eric
26. b—Happy Humphrey
27. a—Jim Wright
28. c—Buddy Rose
29. c—Buddy Rogers
30. a—Paul Bunyan
31. b—Buddy Rogers
32. c—Lansdowne, Ontario
33. c—El Santo
34. c—Ed Lewis
35. c—Bruno Sammartino
36. b—Whipper
37. c—Raphael Halperin
38. c—Ed Lewis
39. d—Master Thomas
40. c—Rocca, Gagne, Thesz
41. b—1937
42. c—Everett Marshall
43. c—Tom Jenkins
44. d—Cobra hold
45. c—Antonino Rocca
46. b—William Cobb
47. c—Georgia
48. a—154-6
49. d—Bill Muldoon
50. a—601 pounds
51. d—Good blood circulation
52. b—Dominick Anthony Galento
53. True
54. d—Bill Longson
55. b—Football
56. d—Antonino Rocca
57. d—Theodore Vetoyanis
58. b—Freddie Blassie
59. b—The Man
60. c—"Rogers Corner"
61. b—Paul Bunyan
62. c—Bruno Sammartino
63. c—George Hackenschmidt
64. d—None of the above
65. b—Jack Wentworth
66. c—Pat O'Connor
67. b—Claw hold
68. True
69. c—Frank Gotch
70. False
71. b—Paul Bunyan
72. c—8' 2"
73. b—Frank Gotch
74. d—George Raymond Wagner
75. c—Bruno Sammartino
76. c—Armstrong Kay
77. c—56
78. b—1932
79. True
80. c—Rube Wright
81. c—Stan Stasiak
82. c—King Cobra
83. d—*The Killer Ape*
84. a—Lloyd Kelsey
85. b—1920-1932
86. c—Gus Sonnenberg
87. c—Antonino Rocca & Buddy Rogers
88. b—Gus Sonnenberg
89. b—The Crying Greek from Cripple Creek
90. b—England
91. c—Vern Gagne
92. False
93. d—Tom Jenkins
94. b—Bob Backlund
95. b—Pat Patterson
96. b—47 seconds
97. d—Lou Thesz
98. c—Stan Stasiak
99. b—Bob Orton Sr.
100. b—Antonino Rocca

PART IV
Women, Blacks, and Midgets

Women, Blacks, and Midgets

1. Slick's recording of ..... became an instant hit.

   a) "Soulman Jive"
   b) "Jive Bro Soul"
   c) "Soul Brother Jive"
   d) "Jive Soul Bro"

2. Linda Dallas and Misty Blue are graduates of The ..... Wrestling School.

   a) Bob Backlund
   b) Killer Kowalski
   c) Verne Gagne
   d) Fabulous Moolah

3. ..... is Lanny Poffo's sister-in-law.

   a) Baby Doll
   b) Lady Maxine
   c) Elizabeth
   d) Missy Hyatt

4. What do Big Momma, Dark Journey, Peggy Sue, and Elizabeth have in common?

   a) They are valets
   b) They are managers
   c) They are wrestlers
   d) They are managers and wrestlers

5. Sir Oliver Humperdink refuses to manage black grapplers.

   True or False?

#8: Matches between midgets are illegal in most states. True or False?
(Photo by Gene Gordon)

6. Identify the "female Jimmy Snuka."

   a) Wendi Richter
   b) Leilani Kai
   c) Nature Girl
   d) Velvet McIntyre

7. During his tenure in the mid-South division, Junkyard Dog engaged in a bitter feud with

   a) Kamala
   b) Butch Reed
   c) Tony Atlas
   d) Ernie Ladd

8. Matches between midgets are illegal in most states.

   True or False?

9. Rocky Johnson hails from

   a) Canada
   b) Washington, D.C.
   c) New York City
   d) Chicago

10. ..... and Koko B. Ware go hand in hand.

   a) Johnny
   b) Birdie
   c) Frankie
   d) Frenchie

11. ..... was an authentic black "Cat."

    a) Larry Hamilton
    b) Ernie Ladd
    c) Rocky Johnson
    d) Rufus R. Jones

12. Lee and Wendi Richter are second cousins.

    True or False?

13. It is Japanese tradition that female wrestlers do not appear on the same card with their male counterparts.

    True or False?

14. ..... wears a heavy iron chain trailing from a collar around his neck.

    a) S.D. Jones
    b) Rocky Johnson
    c) Junkyard Dog
    d) Tony Atlas

15. A 1987 Slammy Award was presented to ..... as the WWF's Woman of the Year.

    a) Sensational Sherri
    b) Wendi Richter
    c) Elizabeth
    d) The Fabulous Moolah

16. Billy the Kid, Little Louis, Little Brutus, and Sonny Boy Hayes all have one thing in common. What is it?

    a) They are black
    b) They are midgets
    c) They are black midgets
    d) They are NWA attractions

17. What is Mr. T's real name?

    a) Leroy Travers
    b) Lawrence Terry
    c) Lawrence Tero
    d) Lincoln Terry

18. Male-female bouts are generally illegal in this country.

    True or False?

19. The Fabulous Moolah runs a training camp for aspiring wrestlers. What is it called?

    a) The Woman's Camp
    b) Camp Moolah
    c) Moolah's Camp
    d) The Fabulous Moolah Wrestling School

20. She calls herself Killer Tomato and that's no joke.

    True or False?

21. The "Rocky" in Rocky Johnson was taken from

    a) Rocky Johnson Sr.
    b) Rocky Bollie
    c) Rocky Balboa
    d) Rocky Graziano

22. Desiree Petersen began her pro wrestling career in

    a) Canada
    b) South America
    c) Europe
    d) Japan

23. What great black boxing champion has not refereed a professional wrestling match?

    a) Joe Frazier
    b) George Foreman
    c) Joe Louis
    d) Muhammad Ali

24. Who has entered the ring as a "former Dallas Cowboys Cheerleader"?

    a) Susan Starr
    b) Wendi Richter
    c) Lelani Kai
    d) Crystal Monroe

25. This grappler is most definitely a Mr. U.S.A.

    a) Rocky Johnson
    b) Norvell Austin
    c) Tony Atlas
    d) Sonny King

#31: P.P. are the initials of what lady grappler? (Photo by Theo Ehret)

26. Who is Mike Jones?

    a) Koko B. Ware
    b) Virgil
    c) Bad Bad Leroy Brown
    d) Sonny King

27. These two women formed one of the few mother-daughter tag teams in the history of grappling. They are

    a) Lee & Wendi Richter
    b) Donna & Doris Day
    c) Debbie & Cora Combs
    d) Peggy & Lisa Lee

28. Ted DiBiase's valet and ..... are one and the same.

    a) Stagger Lee
    b) Charlie Cook
    c) Soul Train Jones
    d) Big Bubba Olsen

29. When did The Fabulous Moolah initially win the women's title?

    a) 1947
    b) 1954
    c) 1957
    d) 1959

30. He can wrestle and speak French. Who is he?

    a) Novell Austin
    b) Koko B. Ware
    c) Jerry Morrow
    d) Charlie Cook

31. P.P. are the initials of what lady grappler?

    a) Penny Peters
    b) Peggy Peterson
    c) Peggy Patterson
    d) Penny Patterson

32. Which of the following is not a true midget moniker?

    a) Little Mr. T
    b) Cowboy Wallace
    c) Haiti Kid
    d) Little Beaver

33. Who was Rocky Johnson's first professional foe?

    a) Firpo Shultz
    b) Firpo Zbyzko
    c) Koko B. Ware
    d) Tony Atlas

34. The birthplace of Despina Mantagas is said to be

    a) Athens, Greece
    b) The Isle of Icaria
    c) The Balkans
    d) Hungary

35. The Black Assassin is really

    a) White
    b) Black
    c) Female
    d) A midget

#40: Who popularized the "cocoa butt"? (Photo by Gene Gordon)

36. Who serves as Moolah's training camp assistant?

    a) Joyce Grable
    b) Crystal Monroe
    c) Donna Christantello
    d) Peggy Lee

37. Ernie Ladd was a gridiron star for what three pro teams?

    a) Giants, Jets, Oilers
    b) Oilers, Chiefs, Jets
    c) Chargers, Oilers, Chiefs
    d) Chargers, Oilers, Packers

38. Who could not be considered a veteran?

    a) Violet Viann
    b) Rose Roman
    c) Penny Banner
    d) Lady Maxine

39. Junkyard Dog was a ..... while in college.

    a) Center
    b) Lineman
    c) Track star
    d) Chess champion

40. Who popularized the "cocoa butt"?

    a) Bobo Olsen
    b) Bobo Brazil
    c) Koko B. Ware
    d) Skull Murphy

41. Lady Maxine and Mad Maxine are one and the same.

    True or False?

42. Koko B. Ware was once a member of the ..... troupe.

    a) Paul Ellering
    b) Jimmy Hart
    c) Paul E. Dangerously
    d) Wendall Weatherbee

43. Pez Whatley equals

    a) Prince
    b) Pistol
    c) Precious
    d) Pounding

44. Experts consider ..... to be the top black athlete in pro wrestling.

    a) Rocky Johnson
    b) Tony Atlas
    c) Butch Reed
    d) Junkyard Dog

45. Lelani Kai was once trained by The Fabulous Moolah.

    True or False?

46. What is the Junkyard Dog's educational background?

    a) High school dropout
    b) High school graduate
    c) College dropout
    d) College graduate

47. Mr. T has a young daughter. What is her name?

    a) Tina
    b) Lisa
    c) Tanya
    d) Missy

48. George Wells and ..... are synonymous.

    a) Mister G
    b) Mister W
    c) Master G
    d) Master W

49. Rip Rogers is a lucky man to have ..... as his valet.

    a) Peggy Sue
    b) Linda Rogers
    c) Brenda Britton
    d) Precious Pearl

50. Identify the senior member.

    a) Koko B. Ware
    b) Norvell Austin
    c) Bobo Brazil
    d) Sweet Brown Sugar

#53: Male midget wrestlers outnumber their female counterparts. True or False? (Photo by Theo Ehret)

51. Vivian Vachon is a native of

    a) Manitoba
    b) Ontario
    c) Paris
    d) Quebec

52. Who is "The Soulman"?

    a) Tony Atlas
    b) Rocky Johnson
    c) Sonny King
    d) Junkyard Dog

53. Male midget wrestlers outnumber their female counterparts.

    True or False?

54. Who is the self-proclaimed "Doctor of Style"?

    a) Tony Atlas
    b) Butch Reed
    c) Slick
    d) Koko B. Ware

55. Who did The Fabulous Moolah defeat for her initial championship title?

    a) Violet Viann
    b) June Byers
    c) Peggy Lee
    d) Rose Roman

56. ..... served as Koko B. Ware's mentor.

   a) Herb Welch
   b) Bobo Brazil
   c) Bruno Sammartino
   d) Bob Welch

57. ..... is not a female Mexican grappler.

   a) Chela Zalazar
   b) Toni Diaz
   c) Reyna Gallegos
   d) Irma Aguliar

58. Who is referred to as the "tall Texan"?

   a) Susan Starr
   b) Wendi Richter
   c) Lady Maxine
   d) Peggy Lee

59. ..... Willie rates as one of America's most popular midget wrestlers.

   a) Little
   b) Big
   c) Coconut
   d) Wee

60. Who did Craig Carson face in his initial pro match?

   a) Steve Keirn
   b) Hulk Hogan
   c) Junkyard Dog
   d) Pedro Morales

61. Sonny King has been both wrestler and manager.

    True or False?

62. Women of Japanese wrestling include all of the following except

    a) Devil Masami
    b) Jaguar Yokota
    c) Tiger Kai
    d) Dump Matsumoto

63. Which of the following has never worn a mask?

    a) Tony Atlas
    b) Koko B. Ware
    c) Stagger Lee
    d) Sweet Brown Sugar

64. Wrestling commentary is her game.

    a) Linda Miceli
    b) Robin McIntyre
    c) Boni Blackstone
    d) Linda Fairchild

65. Mister T made his official pro wrestling debut in Madison Square Garden on March 31, 1985.

    True or False?

#70: ..... is known as "The Indian Star." (Photo by Theo Ehret)

66. What title was at stake in Larry Hamilton's first bout?

   a) Heavyweight
   b) U.S. Junior Heavyweight
   c) World's Junior Heavyweight
   d) Mid-South Heavyweight

67. Tony Atlas has defeated Hulk Hogan.

   True or False?

68. How long did Moolah's reign last?

   a) 37 years
   b) 27 years
   c) 22 years
   d) 30 years

69. Ernie Ladd defeated his first opponent in near-record time. How long did it take?

   a) 55 seconds
   b) 5 seconds
   c) 17 seconds
   d) 45 seconds

70. ..... is known as "The Indian Star."

   a) Princess Victoria
   b) Little Running Flower
   c) Lelani Kai
   d) Susan Starr

71. Select the "Hacksaw" duo.

    a) Ware & Duggan
    b) Atlas & Piper
    c) Reed & Duggan
    d) Valentine & Duggan

72. Scandor Akbar has been associated with

    a) Junkyard Dog
    b) Kamala
    c) Tony Atlas
    d) Charlie Cook

73. Tiny Tim does exist as a pint-sized grappler.

    True or False?

74. ..... earns her living as one of the few women referees in profes-
    sional wrestling.

    a) Linda Carter
    b) Lisa Marie
    c) Rita Marie
    d) Peggy Anne

75. What is Lelani Kai's horoscope sign?

    a) Scorpio
    b) Pisces
    c) Leo
    d) Aquarius

#78: Joyce Grable and ..... won the United States tag team belt in 1976. (Photo by Theo Ehret)

76. In what year did Moolah make her pro debut?

    a) 1954
    b) 1957
    c) 1949
    d) 1959

77. ..... a.k.a. Sweet Brown Sugar.

    a) Tony Atlas
    b) Koko B. Ware
    c) Junkyard Dog
    d) Butch Reed

78. Joyce Grable and ..... won the United States tag team belt in 1976.

    a) Wendi Richter
    b) Vicki Williams
    b) Velvet McIntyre
    c) Carol Haynes

79. Misty Blue Simmes is an atheist.

    True or False?

80. The song "Another One Bites the Dust" has served as whose theme?

    a) Tony Atlas
    b) Butch Reed
    c) Junkyard dog
    d) Ernie Ladd

81. How tall was Ernie Ladd?

    a) 7' 2"
    b) 6' 9"
    c) 6' 2"
    d) 6' 0"

82. June Byers was an Olympic track star prior to entering the professional grappling ranks.

    True or False?

83. Where did Moolah turn pro?

    a) Massachusetts
    b) New York
    c) Florida
    d) South Carolina

84. "Girls Just Want To Have Fun" has been associated with what lady wrestler?

    a) Susan Starr
    b) Peggy Lee
    c) Wendi Richter
    d) Crystal Monroe

85. What woman did not receive a 1987 Slammy nomination?

    a) The Fabulous Moolah
    b) Wendi Richter
    c) Sensational Sherri
    d) Dolly Parton

#88 Midget bouts are the most popular form of professional wrestling. True or False? (Photo by Theo Ehret)

86. The July 1984 promotion which saw Wendi Richter defeat Moolah was billed as

    a) "The Brawl To End It All"
    b) "Wrestlemania I"
    c) "The War To Settle The Score"
    d) "Super Sunday"

87. What wrestler was trained in criminology?

    a) Tony Atlas
    b) Rocky Johnson
    c) Larry Hamilton
    d) Bobo Brazil

88. Midget bouts are the most popular form of professional wrestling.

    True or False?

89. The initials M.L.K. refer to what little fellow of the "squared circle"?

    a) Mighty Little Kenny
    b) Mean Little Kevin
    c) Monsignor Laurence Kelly
    d) Monsoon Lee Kai

90. Lisa Sliaw's maiden name is

    a) Bryers
    b) Evers
    c) Edison
    d) Davis

91. Anita Baker was one of the few black women to wrestle professionally.

    True or False?

92. Which of the following is a women's wrestling organization?

    a) PWC
    b) FCW
    c) WCW
    d) AWF

93. During the early part of her career, The Fabulous Moolah was known as

    a) The Fabulous Fay
    b) The Fabulous Moolah
    c) Slave Girl Moolah
    d) Moolah Baby

94. ..... sported the "Michael Jackson look" when teamed with Koko B. Ware.

    a) Norvell Austin
    b) Craig Carson
    c) Tommy Tune
    d) Sonny King

95. To be a midget, black, and female is something of a rarity in pro wrestling.

    True or False?

96. The Iron Sheik, Butch Reed, One Man Gang, and Nikolai Vol-koff were all managed by Slick.

    True or False?

97. Who is the "Greek Goddess"?

    a) Susan Starr
    b) Lelani Kai
    c) Despina Mantagas
    d) Princess Victoria

98. The dance performed by Koko B. Ware and friend.

    a) The Piledriver
    b) The Stomp
    c) The Slammy
    d) The Bird

99. Kamala is a 360-pound Ghanaian giant.

    True or False?

100. What character did Mr. T portray in *Rocky III*?

    a) Thunderlips
    b) Blackie Blake
    c) Clubber Lang
    d) Thumper Lang

Women, Blacks, and Midgets
the answers

1. d—"Jive Soul Bro"
2. b—Killer Kowalski
3. c—Elizabeth
4. a—They are valets
5. False
6. c—Nature Girl
7. b—Butch Reed
8. False
9. b—Washington, D.C.
10. c—Frankie
11. b—Ernie Ladd
12. False
13. True
14. c—Junkyard Dog
15. c—Elizabeth
16. b—They are midgets
17. c—Lawrence Tero
18. True
19. b—Camp Moolah
20. True
21. b—Rocky Bollie
22. c—Europe
23. b—George Foreman
24. b—Wendi Richter
25. c—Tony Atlas
26. b—Virgil
27. c—Debbie & Cora Combs
28. c—Soul Train Jones
29. c—1957
30. c—Jerry Morrow
31. c—Peggy Patterson
32. b—Cowboy Wallace
33. b—Firpo Zbyzko
34. b—The Isle of Icaria
35. b—Black
36. c—Donna Christantello
37. c—Chargers, Oilers, Chiefs
38. d—Lady Maxine
39. b—Lineman
40. b—Bobo Brazil
41. True
42. b—Jimmy Hart
43. b—Pistol
44. b—Tony Atlas
45. True
46. d—College graduate
47. b—Lisa
48. c—Master G
49. c—Brenda Britton
50. c—Bobo Brazil

51. d—Quebec
52. b—Rocky Johnson
53. True
54. c—Slick
55. b—June Byers
56. a—Herb Welch
57. b—Toni Diaz
58. b—Wendi Richter
59. c—Coconut
60. a—Steve Keirn
61. True
62. c—Tiger Kai
63. a—Tony Atlas
64. c—Boni Blackstone
65. True
66. b—U.S. Junior Heavyweight
67. True
68. b—27 years
69. c—17 seconds
70. a—Princess Victoria
71. c—Reed & Duggan
72. b—Kamala
73. True
74. c—Rita Marie
75. d—Aquarius
76. a—1954
77. b—Koko B. Ware
78. b—Vicki Williams
79. False
80. c—Junkyard Dog
81. b—6' 9"
82. False
83. a—Massachusetts
84. c—Wendi Richter
85. b—Wendi Richter
86. a—"The Brawl To End It All"
87. c—Larry Hamilton
88. False
89. b—Mean Little Kevin
90. b—Evers
91. False
92. c—WCW
93. c—Slave Girl Moolah
94. a—Norvell Austin
95. True
96. True
97. c—Despina Mantagas
98. d—The Bird
99. False
100. c—Clubber Lang

About the Author

ROBERT MYERS was born and raised in The Bronx, New York. He attended Baruch College (B.A.) and Jersey City State College (M.A.). He is currently at work on his first novel, a spy thriller. Mr. Myers resides in New York City with his wife and two children.